THE SAD [illegible]G

retold by **Stan Cullimore**
illustrated by **Justin Grassi**

THE SAD KING

Cast

The King

The Queen

Mike

Ben

Katy

This is the story of a king
who did not smile, did not laugh and
was never, ever silly.

Act One

In the throne room.

The King and Queen are watching TV.

King: *(Sadly)* What is wrong with me?

Queen: I don't know. What is wrong with you?

King: I never smile and I never laugh ... and I'm never silly.

Queen: I know. Now be quiet. I'm trying to watch TV.

King: *(Sighing)* When I was a little boy I would smile and laugh and be silly every day.

Queen: So what? It's much more fun to watch TV every day.

King: No, it's not!

The King suddenly gets up and turns the TV off. The Queen looks cross.

Queen: What did you do that for?

King: Because I want to smile and laugh and be silly.

Queen: You are silly – you turned the TV off!

King: Yes I did, and I won't turn it on again until I have smiled and laughed AND been silly.

The King and Queen look at each other for a few minutes.

Queen: Come on, then. Hurry up and smile. I want to watch TV again.

King: You must smile as well.

Queen: I will smile when you laugh.

King: I will laugh when you are silly.

There is a knock at the door.

King: Come in!

Katy comes in with a bag of doughnuts.

Katy: Good morning, Your Majesty. Would you like a doughnut?

King: *(Sighing)* No, thank you.

Katy: What's wrong, Your Majesty? You look sad!

Queen: He wants to laugh and smile.

Katy: I'm sorry. I haven't got any jokes – just doughnuts.

The King looks at Katy. Suddenly, he jumps up.

King: That's it! Katy, you have given me an idea.

Katy: Me? What idea?

King: We must find a silly joke.

Queen: Why?

King: A silly joke will make me smile and laugh.

Queen: But how will we find a silly joke?

Katy: That's easy. Put an advert on TV.

King: What do you mean?

Katy: Make an advert to ask the people to find you a silly joke.

King: That is another good idea, Katy!

Katy: Thank you, Your Majesty.

Queen: We could ask them to bring their jokes next Friday.

King: And I will give a bag of gold to the person who can make me laugh. Come on! Let's do it at once!

They run out.

Act Two

Friday morning. Ben and Mike are by the palace door. Shouting can be heard behind the door.

Ben: What's all that noise?

Mike: It's the people outside. They saw the advert on TV.

Ben: Oh, yes, so they want to tell the King their jokes.

Mike: Yes. They all want the bag of gold.

Ben: Why don't you let them in?

Mike: Because it's not fair. I want to have that big bag of gold, but I don't know any jokes. What can I do?

They both think. They don't see Katy coming in with her bag of doughnuts.

Mike: I know! I will only let people into the palace if they say they will give me half of what they get from the King.

Ben: Great idea! That way you will get half of the big bag of gold.

Mike opens the door.
The first person comes in.

Mike: I will only let you come in if you will give me half of what you get from the King.

Katy: *(To herself)* This isn't fair! I must put a stop to it.

Katy walks to the throne room.
Ben is by the door.

Ben: Mike has given me an idea, too! Here comes the first person to see the King.

The first person comes up to Ben.

Ben: You can only see the King if you will give me half of what he gives you.

Katy: *(To herself)* Oh, no! He's as bad as Mike. What can I do to stop him?

Act Three

In the throne room.
All the people have told the King their jokes.
Nobody could make him laugh.

King: The people have told me all the jokes they could think of, but the jokes were just not funny.

Queen: No, they were not funny at all!

There is a knock at the door.

King: Come in!

Katy comes in and walks up to the King.

King: *(Sadly)* I don't want any doughnuts, thank you, Katy.

Katy: I haven't come here to give you doughnuts, Your Majesty.

Queen: Then why have you come here?

Katy: To make the King smile.

King: Can you do that?

Katy: I don't know. I have something to ask you first.

King: What is it?

Katy: If I can make you smile, please will you give me two whacks on the nose?

The King looks at the Queen and smiles.

King: But Katy, that is just silly!

Katy: Yes, I know.

Queen: King, you just smiled!

King: So I did! Katy, I just smiled!

Katy: I saw you. Now you can give me two whacks on the nose.

The King stops smiling.

King: Do you really want two whacks, Katy?

Katy: Yes, I do, but before you give them to me, can I ask you to do something?

King: Yes, you can. What is it this time?

Katy: Can you ask Mike and Ben to come in here, please?

King: Yes, I can. Mike! Ben! Come in here.

Mike and Ben come into the room.

Mike: Look, Ben. The King is smiling.

Ben: I know.

Mike: Now we will each get half of that big bag of gold!

Ben: I know.

Katy goes up to Mike.

Katy: Mike, what did I say to you before I came in here to see the King?

Mike smiles.

Mike: You said that if the King gave you something, I could have half of it.

Katy: That's right.

Mike: So where is it then? Come on, hurry up and give it to me.

Katy: I will. Just wait.

Katy goes up to Ben.

Katy: Ben, what did I say to you before I came in here to see the King?

Ben smiles.

Ben: You said that if the King gave you something, I could have half of it.

Katy: That's right.

Ben: So where is it then? Come on, hurry up and give it to me.

Katy: I will. Just wait.

Then the King smiled – a really big smile.

King: Now that is funny.

The King laughs.

King: That is very funny.

He laughs harder and harder.

Queen: What is so funny?

King: Don't you see? Katy has played a trick on these two men. They each want half of what I am going to give her.

Queen: What are you going to give her?

Katy: Two whacks on the nose.

Mike: You mean I get a whack on the nose?

Katy: Yes, so does Ben.

Mike and Ben stop smiling. They look scared.

Mike: I don't want a whack on the nose!

Ben: Nor do I!

Ben and Mike run away.

King: I hope they never come back. Now, I have got something for you, Katy.

Queen: Are you still going to give her two whacks on the nose?

King: No. I'm going to give her a big bag of gold ...

Queen: Good!

King: AND a new job!

Queen: What job is that?

King: Katy, it is your job to make sure that the people who look after me are not greedy.

Katy: Can I still make doughnuts, too?

King: Oh, yes! And now, let's watch some TV.

From that day on, the King was not sad any more. He was happy. He smiled and laughed and was silly all the time ...